EXPLORING OUR UNIVERSE

STARS

LAUREN KUKLA

Checkerboard Library

An Imprint of Abdo Publishing
abdopublishing.com

abdopublishing.com

Published by Abdo Publishing, a division of ABDO, PO Box 398166, Minneapolis, Minnesota 55439. Copyright ©2017 by Abdo Consulting Group, Inc. International copyrights reserved in all countries. No part of this book may be reproduced in any form without written permission from the publisher. Checkerboard Library™ is a trademark and logo of Abdo Publishing.
Printed in the United States of America, North Mankato, Minnesota
102016
012017

THIS BOOK CONTAINS RECYCLED MATERIALS

Design: Emily O'Malley, Mighty Media, Inc.
Production: Mighty Media, Inc.
Editor: Paige Polinsky
Cover Photograph: NASA
Interior Photographs: Getty Images, p. 17; Mighty Media, Inc., pp. 23, 28, 29; NASA, pp. 9, 10, 13, 14, 19, 21, 25, 26, 27; Shutterstock pp. 5, 7; Wikimedia Commons, p. 19

Publisher's Cataloging-in-Publication Data

Names: Kukla, Lauren, author.
Title: Stars / by Lauren Kukla.
Description: Minneapolis, MN : Abdo Publishing, 2017. | Series: Exploring our
     universe | Includes bibliographical references and index.
Identifiers: LCCN 2016944827 | ISBN 9781680784084 (lib. bdg.) |
     ISBN 9781680797619 (ebook)
Subjects: LCSH: Stars--Juvenile literature.
Classification: DDC 523.8--dc23
LC record available at http://lccn.loc.gov/2016944827

CONTENTS

MISSION
EXPLORING SIRIUS

On a clear night, you can see more than 2,000 twinkling stars. You might also see a bright, glowing band. This band is our home **galaxy**, the Milky Way. There are so many stars there, they look like a single glowing streak.

Bright Light

Some stars are brighter than others. But that doesn't mean they're closer to us. Barnard's Star is about 12 **trillion** miles (19 trillion km) from Earth. It is very dim. Sirius is the brightest star in the night sky. But it is more than 51 trillion miles (82 trillion km) away!

More than Meets the Eye

From Earth, stars seem like tiny specks. But they are larger than they appear. Our star, the sun, is 100 times wider than Earth. Other stars are much larger.

There are about 300 billion stars in the Milky Way galaxy.

A Long Journey

Looking at stars is like looking back in time. It takes many years for a star's light to reach Earth. What were you doing eight and a half years ago? That was when the light you see left Sirius.

CHAPTER 1

MEET A STAR

Stars are celestial bodies that produce their own light. The universe contains more than 100 billion **galaxies**. And each galaxy contains billions of stars. That means the universe contains **trillions** of stars!

Stars range in size and brightness. They are all made up mostly of gases. But each star can contain different amounts of elements.

Our sun is an average star. It is medium in size, and its **core** is about 27,000,000 degrees Fahrenheit (15 million°C). That sounds extremely hot. But it is an average temperature for a star. Some stars can burn up to 10 billion degrees Fahrenheit (5.6 billion°C)!

Eight planets orbit our sun. Scientists believe many other stars have planets orbiting them too. But ours is the only solar system known to contain life.

Approximately 1,300,000 Earths could fit inside the sun!

CHAPTER 2

A STAR IS BORN

Stars begin as clouds of gas and dust called nebulae. Nebulae are made of **helium** and **hydrogen** atoms. They also have small amounts of oxygen, **nitrogen**, and more. Gravity forces nebulae to **condense** into smaller clouds. Each cloud may become a star.

It takes millions of years for a star to fully form. First, the collapsing nebula forms a rotating **core** at its center. This core is called a protostar. The protostar's gravity draws more material inward. It eventually flattens into a disk.

As the core flattens, it rotates faster. Its gravity pulls in material from the rest of the cloud. So, the protostar grows very **dense**. As the core condenses, its atoms **collide**. This causes the protostar's temperature to rise.

The group of stars created from the same original nebulae will become a star cluster. The Pleiades star cluster contains more than 600 stars.

A protostar's rotating core works like a spinning figure skater. When the skater has her arms outstretched, she spins slowly. As the skater brings her arms in closer to her body, she spins faster.

Eventually, the protostar reaches about 18 million degrees Fahrenheit (10 million°C). Then something amazing happens. As the **hydrogen** atoms **collide**, their heat fuses them together. This is known as nuclear fusion, and it releases a huge amount of energy.

When two **hydrogen** atoms fuse, they become one **helium** atom. This new atom's mass is less than the mass of the two original atoms. The leftover mass is energy! The star gives off this energy as light and heat.

Some stars never become hot enough for fusion. These stars become brown dwarfs. They glow dimly from their heat. But they never become as bright as our sun.

Once formed, a new star's burning **core** continues to draw gas and dust. This surrounds the core, becoming the star's shell. Over millions of years, leftover shell materials form planets, asteroids, and comets. These smaller objects orbit the star, becoming a solar system.

DID YOU KNOW ?

Scientists believe the sun was born in a star cluster. But it drifted so far from its siblings that they haven't found its birthplace. However, in 2014, scientists discovered a star with a similar age and composition to our sun. They believe it might be our sun's sibling!

CHAPTER 3

STAR DEATHS

Nuclear fusion will power a star for billions of years. But massive stars have shorter life spans than smaller stars. This is because massive stars use up the **hydrogen** fuel in their **cores** more quickly.

When a star's core runs out of hydrogen, nuclear fusion stops. The core then collapses. While collapsing, it grows hotter. The star's hot shell eventually begins a new nuclear fusion cycle. Meanwhile, the core's heat expands the shell. The star becomes a larger star, called a red giant.

Once the star's core reaches 180 million degrees Fahrenheit (100 million°C), it begins burning its **helium**. But after

DID YOU KNOW?

Scientists believe our sun will die in about 5 billion years. But first, it will become a red giant. The sun's expanding shell will swallow up Earth!

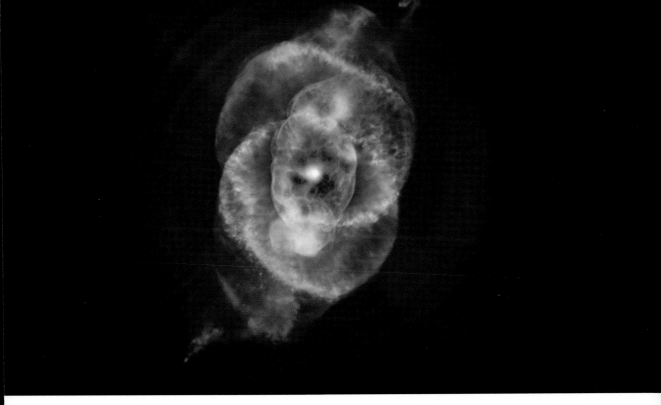

The Cat's Eye nebula is currently collapsing. Scientists believe it will become a white dwarf in a few billion years.

about 100 million years, it runs out of **helium**. The dead star's **core** shrinks to the size of Earth. This is called a white dwarf. The white dwarf cools for billions of years. Then, it becomes a black dwarf. Black dwarfs do not glow.

13

Cassiopeia A is one of the best-known supernovae. One supernova can produce more energy than our sun will produce in its entire lifetime.

Most stars become black dwarfs. But a dying massive star puts on a spectacular show! After burning through its **helium**, its **core** can reach 1 billion degrees Fahrenheit (600 million°C). This heat burns carbon, which creates other elements.

When the carbon supply is gone, the star burns the other elements. This creates even more elements to burn. Eventually, the fusion of elements converts the star's core to iron. This **dense** iron core collapses into a neutron star.

A neutron star is about the size of Manhattan Island in New York City. It is incredibly dense. The rest of the dying star's matter is drawn toward the neutron star's gravity. But the neutron star's atoms are packed so tightly that the matter bounces off the star in a huge explosion! This explosion is called a supernova.

Some stars are so dense that they continue to collapse after becoming a neutron star. Eventually, the star's mass is crushed into a single point. This is called a black hole. Black holes are the densest objects in the universe.

CHAPTER 4

MAPPING THE SKIES

Today, scientists can find black holes and supernovae. But people have observed stars for thousands of years. Ancient people around the world created myths about star constellations. They used these constellations to navigate and track the seasons.

Stars don't change their positions in the sky. But as Earth orbits the sun, these positions appear to change. The appearance of certain stars often match the change of seasons. The only star that seems to have a constant position is Polaris, or the North Star. It always appears directly above the North Pole.

DID YOU KNOW ?

People in the northern and southern hemispheres see different constellations. This is because the curve of the Earth blocks part of the sky.

Hipparchus's star chart was the first of its kind.
It tracked the positions of about 850 different stars.

In about 100 BCE, Greek astronomer Hipparchus charted many stars. He organized them based on brightness. When the telescope was invented in 1608, astronomers discovered many new stars. By the 1800s, they could calculate the distances to these stars. And the 1900s brought even more exciting discoveries.

In the early 1900s, US astronomer Annie Jump Cannon developed a system to classify stars. First, Cannon found a star's spectrum. To do this, she used a telescope **prism**. The prism **refracted** starlight into a band of colors. This was the star's spectrum.

Dark lines divided each color. Cannon compared these lines to spectra from Earth materials. This proved the star contained the same Earth elements. Cannon organized stars based on these lines.

At this time, most astronomers believed stars were rocky bodies, like Earth. But British astronomer Cecilia Payne thought otherwise. She proved that stars were composed mostly of **hydrogen** and **helium**. This meant they were gaseous.

Cannon's system is still used today. And astronomers still use Payne's method to study stars. The work of these two scientists has helped astronomers understand objects **light-years** away.

SUPER SCIENTIST

CECILIA PAYNE

Cecilia Payne was born in Wendover, England, in 1900. As a young woman, she became interested in astronomy. However, women had few scientific opportunities in England. So, in 1923, Payne traveled to Harvard University in Massachusetts. There, she studied astronomy with classmate Annie Jump Cannon.

Payne studied Cannon's data. She used it to prove the temperature and composition of stars. Some scientists said her idea was impossible. Still, Payne published her theory in a book. Astronomers soon accepted it, and her findings still hold true today.

Thanks to Payne, we now know that the sun is made primarily of hydrogen.

CHAPTER 5

MEASURING STARLIGHT

Stars are incredibly far away. Even the most powerful telescopes cannot see their surfaces. But scientists can use starlight to measure a star's distance from Earth.

A star's brightness from Earth is its apparent magnitude. However, magnitude can be misleading. A close star may appear dim because it is small. A faraway star may appear bright because it is large. Because of this, scientists must use **parallax** to find a star's distance.

To determine parallax, astronomers first calculate a star's position in the sky. They do this when the Earth faces one side of the sun. Six months later, they take a second measurement. The star's position will appear to shift. The greater the shift, the farther the star. Astronomers compare a star's apparent magnitude and distance. This determines its parallax.

Sirius A (*left*) is nicknamed the Dog Star. Its smaller neighbor, Sirius B (*right*), is sometimes called the Pup.

CHAPTER 6

FAR, FAR AWAY

Many stars are too far away to track using **parallax**. Astronomers use stellar spectra to estimate their distances. A star's spectrum indicates its temperature. This temperature reveals the star's actual brightness, or absolute magnitude.

Scientists count backward when they measure magnitude. This means the lower a star's magnitude, the brighter it is. Astronomers compare the absolute magnitude to the apparent magnitude. They use this information to estimate the star's distance.

Stellar distances are measured in **light-years**. One light-year is about 5.9 **trillion** miles (9.5 trillion km). The universe is so huge that stars in our own **galaxy** can be 700,000 light-years away. Polaris is about 323 light-years away. Its light is 323 years old when it reaches Earth!

POLARIS
323 light-years from Earth

**PROXIMA
CENTAURI**
4.2 light-years from Earth

MARS
12.6 light-minutes from Earth

SUN
8.3 light-minutes from Earth

MOON
1.3 light-seconds from Earth

EARTH

Our universe is incredibly vast! One light-second is
about 186,000 miles (300,000 km). One light-minute
is about 11 million miles (18 million km).

CHAPTER 7

TRIP TO THE STARS

Visiting another star system is a distant dream. But in 1990, the Hubble Space Telescope (HST) began orbiting Earth. Since then, it has taken images of distant **galaxies** and nebulae. It has helped scientists understand where stars first came from.

The National Aeronautics and Space Administration (**NASA**) is currently building a new telescope. It is called the James Webb Space Telescope. When complete, it will be the world's most powerful telescope. It may allow us to see stars in more distant galaxies.

We can't visit the stars ourselves. But our spacecraft can. In 1977, NASA launched two **probes**. They were called *Voyager 1* and *Voyager 2*. The probes first explored the planets Jupiter, Saturn, Uranus, and Neptune. Then they sailed toward the edge of the solar system.

TOOLS OF DISCOVERY

SPACE TELESCOPE IMAGING SPECTROGRAPH

In 1997, a Space Telescope Imaging Spectrograph (STIS) was added to the HST. Like Payne's prism, it separates starlight. The STIS spreads the light into a spectrum. This spectrum shows different types of light waves. But the STIS does not just work on visible light. The STIS is also able to separate ultraviolet light and some infrared light. This gathers information about the star's distance, temperature, and motion.

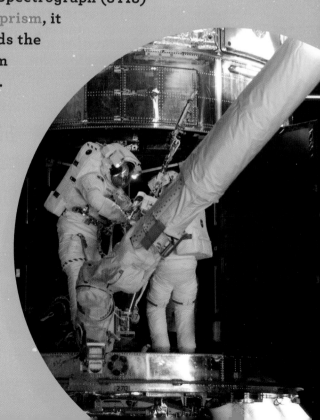

In 2009, two astronauts repaired the STIS. The spacewalk took more than eight hours!

In 2013, *Voyager 1* entered **interstellar** space. *Voyager 2* will soon leave the solar system too. In 2020, both **probes** will run out of power. They will no longer communicate with our scientists. But they will continue to drift through space. Eventually, they will pass by distant stars.

Our current spacecraft would take many lifetimes to reach a star. That means no human could survive a trip to one. Still, some scientists believe that future interstellar travel might be possible. Engineers are trying to build faster spacecraft. Other scientists are studying ways humans could sleep over the long journey.

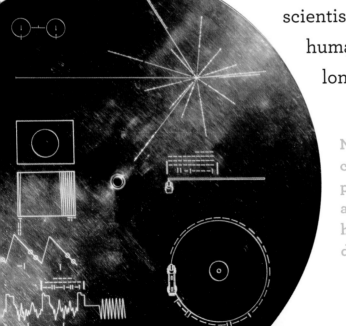

NASA included a gold-plated copper disk on each *Voyager* probe. The disks contain sounds and images of life on Earth. NASA hopes the probes might one day be discovered by an alien species.

Voyager 1 consists of 65,000 individual parts. It cost $865 million to build the spacecraft.

Our machinery must improve before we can become **interstellar** travelers. Until then, scientists study faraway stars through telescopes. What they learn helps us understand our solar system's past, as well as its future.

STELLAR GUIDEBOOK

Brightest Stars

Sun

- Constellation: None
- Distance from Earth:
93 million miles
(150 million km), or
8 light-minutes
- Absolute Magnitude: 4.8

Sirius

- Constellation:
Canis Major
- Distance from Earth:
8.6 light-years
- Absolute Magnitude:
1.42

Canopus

- Constellation: Carina
- Distance from Earth:
313 light-years
- Absolute Magnitude:
−5.65

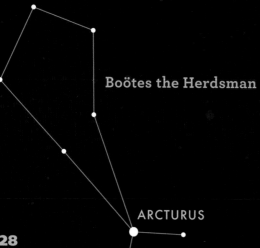

Boötes the Herdsman

ARCTURUS

Arcturus

- Constellation: Boötes
- Distance from Earth: 36.7 light-years
- Absolute Magnitude: −0.30

Alpha Centauri (Triple-Star System)

- Consists of Alpha Centauri A, Alpha Centauri B, and Proxima Centauri
- Constellation: Centaurus
- Distance from Earth: 4.2–4.4 light-years

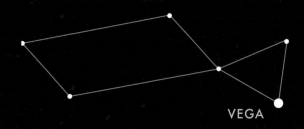

Lyra the Harp

VEGA

- Absolute Magnitude:
4.38 (Alpha Centauri A)
5.71 (Alpha Centauri B)
15.6 (Proxima Centauri)

Vega

- Constellation: Lyra
- Distance from Earth: 25 light-years
- Absolute Magnitude: 0.58

GLOSSARY

collide — to come together with force.

condense — to make more compact.

core — the central part of a celestial body, usually having different physical properties from the surrounding parts.

dense — thick or compact.

galaxy — a very large group of stars and planets.

helium — a light, colorless gas that does not burn.

hydrogen — a gas with no smell or color that is lighter than air and catches fire easily.

infrared — energy transmitted by waves, which can be felt as heat.

interstellar — located, taking place, or traveling outside our solar system.

light wave — an amount of light energy that travels through air or water in the shape of a wave. A wavelength is the distance between one point on a wave and the next.

light-minute — the distance that light travels in one minute.

light-second — the distance that light travels in one second.

light-year — the distance that light travels in one year.

NASA — National Aeronautics and Space Administration. NASA is a US government agency that manages the nation's space program and conducts flight research.

nitrogen — a colorless, odorless, tasteless gas. It is the most plentiful element in Earth's atmosphere and is found in all living matter.

parallax — the difference in apparent direction of an object as seen from two different points not on a straight line with the object.

prism — a clear solid glass or plastic shape that breaks up light into the colors of the spectrum.

probe — device used to explore and send back information.

refract — to change the path of light rays as they pass from one medium to another.

trillion — the number 1,000,000,000,000, or one thousand billion.

WEBSITES

To learn more about Exploring Our Universe, visit booklinks.abdopublishing.com. These links are routinely monitored and updated to provide the most current information available.

INDEX